# A Reason to Show Up for Work Tomorrow Morning

# A Reason to Show Up for Work Tomorrow Morning

## Dedication To Outstanding Workplace Heroes

Cynthia  A. Jenkins

| Library of Congress Control Number: | | 2007902473 |
| --- | --- | --- |
| ISBN: | Hardcover | 978-1-4257-5138-8 |
| | Softcover | 978-1-4257-5137-1 |

This book was printed in the United States of America.

**To order additional copies of this book, contact:**
Xlibris Corporation
1-888-795-4274
www.Xlibris.com
Orders@Xlibris.com
37778

# CONTENTS

# DEDICATION

To All employees and individuals, past and present,

who go the daily distance to *serve people*,

in Clayton County

# A Reason to Show Up for Work Tomorrow Morning

*A Dedication to Workplace Heroes*

# FOREWORD

Many have described county employees as lazy, half-working, or taking it easy because they have a job for life. However, when I worked for Clayton County, Georgia, I worked with outstanding teammates and leaders. Many of these people were the most industrious examples I had ever met upclose. Therefore, I never understood those descriptions. Let me tell you about the magistrate clerk who answers the phone before 7:00 a.m. Or the legal assistants who come in at 6:00 a.m. just to complete paperwork so that they can focus more on the public by 8:00 a.m. Or the bailiff that welcomes you to the courthouse with the utmost degree of dignity and respect. Let us not forget the defense attorneys who take time out to make you feel that you matter. Because of these and so many other outstanding examples, I beg to differ with anyone who feels that government employees hardly work.

There are individuals that exert five-star efforts each day despite the ever-prominent example like Enron. For example, in the past, our parents worked for one company their entire lives and then retired with a nice great package. Further, they were responsible for one job. Today, the term "multitasking" has become very commonplace. So why do today's employees continue to give their best? What are the rewards for doing a good job other than retirement? What makes people not roll in at work late, but show up far in advance, say, at 8:00 a.m.? Why would a person report early in a time when work has become much more demanding than years ago?

They show up day after day after day because they have strong work ethics. For these individuals, it is not merely enough to maintain a job; they want to excel at it and give it their best efforts. True, they may not make millions or receive a lot of kickbacks. However, when these individuals lay their heads down at night, they can sleep with a good conscience knowing they've contributed their *best* for the benefit of the public.

So what about you? Are you an employee searching far and wide to find a reason to get up for work in the morning? Have the new trends of multitasking and downsizing and the lack of company loyalty moved you to want to turn off the alarm, roll over, and stay at home? Are you a manager seeking for a way to motivate and retain your best employees? If you feel any of these, this book will give you the motivation you need to get up and face the day. Plus, it will help you to not only identify the modern-day heroes working at your side, but show you how to become an extraordinary hero for others.

# CHAPTER 1

# *Why a Government Office?*

How did you feel the last time you paid a visit to a government office to get your driver's license or handle some other matter? Is this one of your favorite things to do? Probably not. When I arrived at the county, I came with a preconceived notion about a government office. In fact, I had heard many stories of workers lacking the readiness to serve others. I did not want to be the same way. My goal? To be of benefit to the public and surprise them with an unexpected quality of service. This attitude, plus the teachers and the mentors of the county, made my work experience with government agencies rewarding.

When people are willing to pave the way for new employees in the legal environment, they become incredible heroes. Such heroes create a win for the public and an energetic place to work. There are many ways to mentor and teach.

## What Does an Outstanding Teacher Look Like?

A teacher could be the boss with great leadership qualities who courageously takes a stand for what is right. These people excel at making it worth your while to show up for work. Their examples reveal important aspects of a good working environment. Listen closely and you'll hear the rallying calls: how was your weekend? Can I help you locate a file? Can I work the front desk while you get your work done? Allow me to mail that package out for you. Wow! You look great today. You are so resourceful. Thanks for the suggestions! How could we have done it without you? We need to move you to an area that allows you to use your skills to the fullest.

Any person who treats employees with dignity and respect and makes them feel important enough to be heard would be considered a workplace hero. They are not afraid to share their admiration with others. Their respect for people moves them to honor others. They require themselves to deliver outstanding public service. I consider these to be prerequisites of any public servant.

# CHAPTER 2

## The Solicitor General's Office

For twelve years, I experienced the privilege of working for the county. Coming from the corporate world, I knew I was not in Kansas anymore when my supervisors placed a high priority on family. For example, they made it clear that family comes first. In the event of a family emergency, I was to speak up about it and know that my superiors would respect these emergencies. Over the years, some attorneys have wondered, "How did you succeed in working for the government?" I always thought of myself as working for *people*. Each person was accorded dignity and respect to the best of my ability. As one boss always encouraged, "Treat all people with dignity and respect until they prove they are not worthy of such."

What happens when you fail to treat people with dignity and respect? Well, have you ever had someone walk past you as if you were not standing there? Did you feel dignified and respected? May we never become so busy we just walk past people without saying a word. How important to put forth the effort by saying "Good morning" or giving a quick nod of the head or even a brief smile. Welcome people to the office and wish them a good day. These are very simple and common courtesies. Although these will not cost us a dime, they will go a long way with the public and coworkers. So make the better investment in people. One of my best experiences was working with an incredible team.

# CHAPTER 3

# *A High-Performance Team*

In school, I loved soccer, basketball, field hockey, and baseball. I always loved winning the game. However, it was not due to my skill alone that we won; it was because we had a dynamic team that worked together to get the win. Although we possessed an array of skills, we practiced and clearly communicated our expectations every day. We strived not to beat one another down when we failed to measure up, but to be good coaches and help all reach their highest potential. The exercise of innovative team efforts did not end with school.

## My Mothers of Clayton

It was a privilege to work with three of the most hardworking people I have ever met. We were all legal assistants assigned to various courtrooms. Because of our unique schedules, when one was not present, another would take the place of the other and do whatever was required to get the job done from start to finish. Why was this a privilege for me? Our team was composed of women from varied backgrounds. You didn't see carbon copies of people, but unique individuals with great ideas and perspectives. Therefore, we learned from one another. All three possessed a wealth of experience, not only in the legal field, but also in the field of life. For a person like me who always thought I loved people and never took them for granted, these women taught me to look a little closer and listen a little longer. You will find their stories incredible. They remind me of travels with my aunts as a little girl. I loved listening to their stories of determination and perseverance from the backseat of the car as we traveled between the East and West coasts.

During our travels to training conferences and at early-morning breakfast, my coworkers took me back to that time of long ago. Their intelligence and experience merit an audience. On many occasions, they brought breakfast to me or hauled me down for a cup of coffee, biscuits, and eggs. I generally move at warp speed. So, this was a perfect combination. I can still hear them saying, "Cynthia, sit down and have breakfast and conversation with us" or "Cynthia, we have questions or something very important we need to discuss. Come sit down." Yes, at the start of the day, it was their routine to first see how each other were doing then start the day. In fact, these women would come in extra early to have a short breakfast and talk about a few important things in life before starting the day. Do you sense that warm feeling of family? I grew to admire that and worked toward encouraging it. Although we no longer work together, we still make it a habit to meet for breakfast and have good conversation during the early-morning hours.

Good communication was very important to these teammates. So we had regular meetings too. However, for the most part, these were not the typical "everyone report to the boardroom" meetings. Most were held right on the spot inside a cubicle; others, in alternative offices. We had working breakfasts and lunches at area restaurants. Some were held at 5:15 a.m. This enabled us to come together face-to-face and discuss matters important to the team. Here again I learned a very important lesson about communication. Today's business leaders have a wealth of technology at their disposal, including e-mail, teleconference, or video conference. These tools can help one conduct business while saving time and money. However, the most effective leaders choose the tool of communication most appropriate to *reach the heart* of their team. As communication is a two-way street, a team leader needs to devote time to listening and discernment. So I understood when these three heroes requested face-to-face communication and I honored them accordingly.

Another area that made us all effective is the ability to know the assets of each individual team member. Companies have members that are creative, analytical, process oriented and even natural born leaders. Regardless of the teams' skill sets an intuitive leader will conduct an audit of all skills and assets. If one is wise enough to conduct this evaluation prior to a project, they will receive the ability to assign the right people to the most appropriate job.

During graduate studies, I recognized the value of respecting talents for all team members. Our SGO team was effective because we *lived* by this standard. Therefore, whenever this high-performance team had to present a presentation, create a business proposal, organize a department event, brainstorm for a meeting, or structure a training process, we recognized the strengths of the team and dignified each member with the best assignment. Such consideration created an additional buy-in for that individual to bring the most outstanding work to the table. By conducting such planning on the front end, trusting all members to get their jobs done, we saved time and created masterpieces together.

Even the best teams will encounter problems or misunderstandings. What makes or breaks a team is how each individual player chooses to handle the situation. Will the person prove to be an ethical leader? Will each player assume collective accountability for the team? Because this team respected one another, we never had to worry about receiving secondhand information regarding a problem with their courtroom or responsibilities. Nor was this viewed as an opportunity to exalt ourselves while looking down on the other. We respected one another too much to take that route. Notice the beauty of ethical leadership in action: a team member communicated the situation immediately to the member of focus. If necessary, we contacted our teammate directly at home. This gave her an opportunity to choose an action to remedy the situation. If we could not locate our colleague, we did the ethical thing—*just took care of it*—and, the next day, let them know privately and respectfully how we resolved it. *Collectively* we became whatever we needed to be to support one another and represent our department well. Overall, what I appreciated the most about our team was this: *we did not always agree on everything, but we were willing to learn from one another.*

Because we considered and valued the opinions of all, together we delivered a combination of strengths to the table. Interestingly, they always wanted me to take the lead to request permission to go to conferences or for other special requests. As the senior legal assistant, I did this for a while; however, I knew them to be intelligent women with great ideas and wisdom. So there came a point when I encouraged them to speak up about these requests on their own. Just as they had encouraged me to grow, I learned to encourage them. It is my *privilege* to introduce you to this team.

**BJ Schofill** valued justice for all people. This woman not only possessed a wealth of leadership, but we both shared the value of delivering good customer service. We often outlined this priority to the corporate offices. This habit ensured better customer service for the customer of the future. Mrs. Schofill always highlighted the importance of speaking up for yourself and your teammates. In one sitting, this person could show you how much to save for retirement and where to find the best investments. She is married to a good man of character. For over twenty-five years, she worked for the county of Clayton, giving her best for people everyday.

**Sandra Schofill**, BJ's sister, is a very compassionate mother to all. If you ever meet Sandra, you would know she lives by the golden rule: "Treat others as you would like to be treated." This quality alone contributes to a level of professionalism uncommon in many businesses. Sandra is the type of employee that doesn't require you to beg her to do anything. Whenever any of us were preparing to go on vacation, it was always our understanding to leave that person alone to get their desk cleared. Whatever the person didn't finish, we came over as a group and lent a hand to pick up wherever she left off. We worked as a team to keep the vacationer's desk clear while she was away. Often we gave priority to our team player's desk while addressing our work last. Although many seek to honor Sandra, her greatest reward comes from getting her job done.

**Patricia Orrell** is the heart that loves and welcomes you to the office. This lady will shower you with personalized gifts you did not expect. Although her heart may bubble forth more than she would like to do on certain occasions, you have to appreciate her for her overwhelming compassion for people. Whenever I underwent sickness she always brought something good to eat and read.

Yes, they were a great team and example for all, not only for their gifts of dignity, but also for their unique example of strong work ethic in action. Just as a relay runner in the Olympics carries the token on to the next runner, these ladies would pass the token or assignment to the next player, doing whatever was required to get the job done. Now, along with two new team players, they continue to run like this on a daily basis. I could not have excelled at my job without their consistent support. These ladies represent three compelling reasons to get up and go to work in the morning.

# CHAPTER 4

## *Quiet Leadership*

Within the Victim Services Department dwells the kind, warm, yet professional advocate, **Melanie Woodall**. She has been with the county for over eight years. On a daily basis, she gives time to victims and anyone requiring assistance. This woman has a strong appreciation for her work family. Each day she shares and exhibits those values among the people, especially the public, which she has the privilege to serve.

Although she is very quiet, she exhibits a strong example of positive leadership in word and deed. Victims come to the office every day—downtrodden or seeking relief from abusive situations. Many have endured for so long that they don't know how to leave. This quiet heroine is the perfect welcoming committee to help victims begin the steps to get a measure of relief and freedom from traumas affecting their lives. What an incredible privilege it was to work with this amazing person. Every day I looked forward to seeing her smile. I also enjoyed watching her quiet display of leadership in action. With the greatest amount of certainty, I have no doubt she will keep up the good work.

Another privilege was that of working with **Jenitha Gooch.** From the very first moment, this heroine had a vision to not only outline a plan of action for victims in Clayton County, but to take the program to another level. If you ever meet Jenitha, you will automatically sense her passion for people. She has a desire to make a positive difference. For example, one of her goals is to help victims develop life-development skills.

The Solicitor General's Office (SGO) afforded us both an opportunity to review a wealth of outstanding grants. These programs provide resources and options to victims in difficult circumstances. When you look at Jenitha, you cannot leave her without appreciating her sense of caring for people. May she always have her heartfelt passion for people of the community and the desire to make a positive difference. She gave me a great reason to show up for work in the morning.

Lastly, I have to relate the privilege of working with **Marcus Pittman**. He is an outstanding investigator, who is also a quiet leader. This team player's timely response to requests gave us the freedom to handle emergencies with ease. It was his custom to honor and dignify all employees. Our favorite conversations were about jazz. He would always encourage me to use my money to buy a top-notch stereo for myself. One morning, he and his wife arrived at my office, surprising me with a new stereo. However, it was not just any old stereo; they took the time to set it to my favorite jazz station. What a great investigator and person! By displaying such excellent qualities, he provided a profound reason to show up for work in the morning.

## Team Players with Different Personalities

The Clayton Solicitor General's Office (SGO) was a great place to cultivate people skills. The incredible interactions with people made the difference.

In the years prior to the SGO, I spent a large part of my career working for corporate. I am thankful for what corporate taught me about professionalism, international business and finance. However, it was quite a change in gears to become immersed into a new environment of down-to-earth people who provided a learning experience and an opportunity to use my skills in other effective areas. I will never forget my appointment as a terminal agency coordinator. In the beginning, I had no idea of what my responsibilities would include. However, with the assistance of leaders in the trade it was easy. So with their help and availability along the way, it proved to be a rewarding experience. I loved it!

My success in this position could not have been accomplished without the right hand of the world's best accusation specialists, **Karen Keith** and **Brenda Lowry**. When the new manuals were created, this team always made themselves available to review new training and user manuals *at my request*. However, because they were closest to the job, I was anxious to know their perspectives. These heroes possess the talents of concise and accurate writing abilities. I knew they could help me get the project right for our department. Sometimes, employers fail to ask the people who do the work for their opinion. When employers neglect to create manuals according to an employee's learning style, the user will fail to use the new tools and will simply fall back on what they know, the old and most convenient way of doing things.

Their perspectives proved to be resourceful and insightful. Karen and Brenda are also mothers. Since the first day I walked into the office, they have always been willing to take time to show me, or anyone else, *the way*. What a privilege to have team players that not only hoped the best for you, but sacrificed time to help you to *become* the best.

# CHAPTER 5

## *The Defense Attorneys*

In the prosecutor's office, there is always an ongoing joke that the prosecutors reside on the side of the light and defense on the side of the dark. Defense, of course, might invite you to come from the side of the dark to the light. All jokes set aside, I found both sides to be professional. Both study the facts, presenting them in court in an effort to procure justice. Many came to the office for assistance with clients' cases, and we were glad to give it. However, the best attorneys always took a moment to see how things were going in our lives.

In addition, they shared their latest and greatest plans to help other people within the community. This quality always impressed me. Many enter the field of law to be of assistance to others. Individuals with such decent motives tend to help others and prosper while they are at it. When I first made the transition from business/technology to the legal field, they always exhibited such patience. I think this is why later, when I saw new attorneys walk through the door, it was always my goal to help them become acclimated. Regardless of the level of experience, there is always more to learn and share.

Many defense attorneys proved to be heroes on a number of levels. Notice some of the following outstanding examples.

*"He loves technology and innovation."*

**Frank T. Smith** is *one* of the most ethical attorneys you will ever meet. Not only does he work tirelessly into the night to look out for his clients, but he is always on the lookout for the best innovation to facilitate that process. Furthermore, he volunteers in the community for a number of speaking engagements, all with the goal of mentoring others. One of our favorite discussions was how to run a more efficient business.

Although I had never worked for the defense, our conversations about what the law firm of the future may look like proved to be an eye-opening experience. We often discussed the tools required of an effective trial attorney and the technical structures of various jurisdictions. Therefore, when I later arrived to the side of the defense, I tried to remember his teaching when I worked to develop an organized routine to assist my trial attorney. Instead of making the work harder, it was my goal to simplify the process so the attorney could focus on what he does best, practice law.

Lastly, Frank Smith always made people feel like a winner, often leaving phone messages of gratitude for my hard work. Later, I discovered he is also a leader. How so? Well, Frank never held back from offering commendation privately or publicly. For example, once, while completing an assignment, Mr. Smith made the announcement, "If Cynthia is on the project, I know it will be done!"

Sometimes we may hold back from giving the appropriate commendation to the people who deserve it the most. Frank provided valuable reasons to move beyond ourselves, help others to become their best, and provide a powerful reason to show up for work in the morning.

*"He always found a way to make you laugh."*

Because the field of law is very demanding, it is always a joy to encounter an attorney with a sense of humor. I first met **Mr. Rolf A. Jones** over fourteen years ago. He arrived at the Solicitor's Office with the utmost degree of confidence regarding his client's innocence. Of course, he reconsidered after he saw the long criminal history fly down the hallway. He accepted this knowledge with the greatest degree of humility and sense of humor.

Trial attorneys are incredible! I have personally watched attorneys fresh out of law school complete a great amount of research for a case, but once they walk into the courtroom before a judge and jury, they discover the answer to the question, what am I really made of? Courtroom experience will transform mental fat into muscle. Mr. Jones is one of the most outstanding defense attorneys I have ever had the privilege of witnessing in court.

As a trial attorney, he is required to run to different municipalities on a daily basis, maintain office appointments, and provide access for his firm. When I worked as the assistant to Mr. Jones, my daily role was comparable to that of a legal air traffic controller, so to speak. As a natural-born motivator, my requests consisted of run here, stop by there, pick this up, visit this client, return to the judge's office, etc. The main objective of our journey was to get it all done. Having worked on both sides of the law, I can truly say the most effective attorneys provide their legal assistant's accessibility to the court first thing in the morning to provide coordination of daily appointments, facilitate interface with the court, manage clients, and notify them of any changes in the weather or court that might affect the schedule.

Despite this busy schedule, Mr. Jones has not forgotten to give back to the community he came from, Clayton County. He always shows a special willingness to teach new attorneys and interns. Interestingly, Mr. Jones previously served as a legal secretary. Therefore, it was from this perspective that he maintained his consistency and effectiveness as a mentor. The best attorneys live by these qualities. Maybe one day he will teach classes showing other new graduates not only how to conduct themselves within the court, but also how to mentor, grow, and not lose their sense of humility. I will always remember his kindness in allowing me to gain my first experience working within a small law firm. Like any good coach, he gave knowledge openhandedly and in digestible amounts. These are incredible reasons to show up for work.

## *"A humble attorney with a great appreciation for people!"*

Have you ever met a great attorney? One who did not know how great they were? When I first met **Christine A. Van Dross**, I admired her passion for taking care of her clients and discussing positive ideas. During an interview, I asked Ms. Van Dross to describe the positive things she wanted to bring to Clayton. Notice her vision: "As a leader, I had a desire to provide lawyers who have integrity and compassion. However, my vision did not stop with our representation. Our daily goal was to create a work environment where people wanted to show up for work. Employees spend more time at work than with families. Some work situations require employees to count down the hours until 5:00 p.m. I didn't want any employee to feel that way in our office."

Ms. Van Dross is a person who wants to save every person in the world. In this endeavor, she makes a daily contribution by creating a solid foundation to promote a successful work family. Ms. Van Dross hires employees with good character because these qualities translate into a positive work environment where all employees recognize, respect, and honor the differences of all. As stated earlier, what makes or breaks a team is how each individual player chooses to handle daily situations. Will the person prove to be an ethical leader? Will they consider the personality of the employee and choose an appropriate approach? At the end of the day, does the employee still have a fair amount of dignity? Every day Ms. Van Dross and her league of leaders work together to create a positive and healthy environment to benefit all employees. Sometimes only high-level executives receive cheers, applause, or commendation for outstanding performance. However, Ms. Van Dross did not follow the status quo. Whenever any employee did something good, all employees gathered around, clapped loudly, and honored the person to show "You are worthy." Moreover, she gives the person a special hat that reads, "I'm a winner!" How thoughtful and fun!

This leader is also a great mentor. Because the office has forged a partnership with a college, they have the privilege of working with a number of students. Sometimes students are brought in to do the grunt work or low-prestige jobs. However, Ms. Van Dross has taken their training to a different level. These students are involved in every aspect of the business—from entering state-required data into the computer for court-appointed cases to assisting attorneys, visiting clients in jail, and assisting in court. Every intern in her office receives a well-rounded experience that will increase the marketability of students for the future. Not only does this system help students bring a measure of substance to the workplace, but also it helps regular staff to focus on what they do best. During such training, it is her custom to locate a diamond in the rough. These individuals receive the first consideration when an opportunity of full-time employment becomes available. Because all employees strive for positive leadership, all receive a sense of empowerment. Interns experience the benefit of full involvement within the business. Managers strive to be ethical leaders to inspire staff to greater heights. Lastly, all employees receive an opportunity for advancement to management within their own team environments. Ms. Van Dross makes it a point to dignify and appreciate all employees for their wealth of talents. For example, Olivia Hollowell, with her way of bringing love to the office in a form of a dish, is just one of the outstanding members of Christine's top-notch team. Because Ms. Van Dross is a great attorney, leader, and mentor, she works together with her incredible league of employees to generate outstanding reasons to show up for work every day.

*"James and Kathleen never take kindness for granted."*

Some attorneys consistently display a great disposition and find special ways to express their thanks. One such attorney comes to mind—**James**

**Studdard.** He and his wife/secretary, Kathleen, always remembered the legal assistants and will, even on their vacations. These heroes took advantage of every opportunity to honor others. These are the things I cherish about James and Kathleen. By their example, they taught me a very valuable lesson; to wit, never take kindness or goodness for granted. True heroes in the legal field appreciate and show genuine recognition for the services that people perform. James and Kathleen fit that description. There is no obligation on their part to do anything for us; in fact, it was our job to do the things we do for them. I say this about them to demonstrate that they cared enough about us to dignify our work, thus giving us compelling reasons to show up for work in the morning.

As an aside, James is somewhat of a Renaissance man. He writes weekly editorials for several newspapers, has published and performed plays in the area, speaks Spanish, and, notwithstanding his rigorous and demanding schedule, finds time to be kind and appreciative. Such a refreshing combination!

Other attorneys are great at relating history. Their stories and facts can make you wonder, "How did I miss that in school?" There are many outstanding mentoring attorneys. If this book could transcend into eternity, I would have accepted interviews from all these other heroes. All furnished solid-gold reasons to get up and go to work, ready for action.

# CHAPTER 6

# The Courage to Grow

One of my adopted fathers always encouraged me to face change fearlessly and head-on. When we fail to grow, we can start to look like a part of the furniture. How does this happen? Fear may keep us inside our comfort box or camping out behind the starting line. Maybe we even fail to map out a plan. In the end, there is actually no difference between you and the chair, the rug, or the desk. Furniture cannot change; people often choose not to. One thing I have learned about embracing change is its ability to define *who* you are and then make you a *stronger and better* person. The rhythms of life change every day. I crossed that starting line by deciding to learn the Portuguese language, volunteer within the Brazilian community and return to school to complete educational requirements. My observation of adult education reveals a path of mentors passionate about ethical leadership, teamwork, and organizational success. Many may work as top-notch managers in the field of business. Yet, they have not forgotten the importance of humility and helping others to see their strengths, not weaknesses only. I would not have completed my major in business management without these prerequisites. All of these moves helped me to step out of the box.

So although it was hard to leave a good job, I had to keep growing. Over the years, I have made it a practice to give encouragement so many others may keep growing, fearlessly face change, and strive to reach their full potential. Therefore, it was about time I followed my own advice.

I will always value the gifts gained from both the prosecutor and defense sides. First, the prosecutorial perspective afforded me a wealth of treasures. One was that of learning the structure of the justice system. Another was the ability to manage a large caseload efficiently without sacrificing an appreciation for people. Added to these was the opportunity to learn from some of the best legal minds and mentors I have ever met up close. The defense gave a perspective to see the whole picture and the work required to serve the client. In addition, I gained the privilege of learning the ins and outs of other jurisdictions throughout the Atlanta area. The appreciation for people is essential to nurture client relationships. However, under the mentorship of my defense attorney, I gained the opportunity to ponder *why* we draft motions or any other pleadings and learned how to consider all facts of a case. I have a new appreciation for an organized trial notebook. Both perspectives placed me in a strong position to address the needs of clients and citizens.

Most of all, I value the importance of people skills. The array of different personalities helped me to appreciate that all are raised differently and, therefore, bring various *experiences* to the workplace. Some people will bring more consideration and thoughtfulness than expected, while others will bring A+ personalities combined with high expectations. Some will bring a new level of organization and simplification, while others may prefer to have stuffed animals or a wealth of pictures on their desk because these things make their area feel like home. Some will have a great sense of family. Others will need to learn how to govern themselves within a workplace family. Many are college graduates with a wealth of knowledge. Some never attended college yet are incredibly intelligent. Some will prefer to sit quietly in the background, while others will bring more creativity to a project. Some will require a wealth of directions. Others will hit the ground running. Regardless, all are here because together they bring an incredible amount of value to the workplace. So how did we effectively harness and honor these incredible skills at the Solicitor General's Office?

One of the greatest joy's in life is that of being a unique individual. Therefore, our goal was not to create robots. On the contrary, the key was to try to look for ways to bring a team together. If a business leader wants a successful office, this is the road that must be traveled. How fortunate I was to encounter such variety and combined leadership all in one place. This environment showed me how to respect the individuality of each employee. Without such, it is virtually impossible to manage successfully any relationship or business effectively and graciously.

Another gift I will carry with me is the need to make work rewarding. The Solicitor General's Office outlined the decorum to motivate people to value and appreciate their good work. Work should never feel like a chore. If people have to spend eight hours a day together, *please make some part of it fun.* Leaders of organizations should always be asking, Where is the fun? Do my employees know their value? Could we plan more appreciation lunches? Have I told my employees the difference they make in our company? If employers do these things, employees will respond with gratitude and loyalty.

In fact, every employee is responsible for generating positive energy in the workplace. When the three legal assistants and I showed up early for work, we always dedicated certain songs to each day, especially on Fridays. In fact, on some days, we would take turns allowing each to play their song of choice. At the same time, we created a *fun* workplace. These and others are ways to pick one another up and get the work of the day done!

Although I no longer have the privilege of working with these heroes, I will carry the value for people with me. Returning to school and volunteering in the community has helped me to refine people skills and better show value for differences. Thank you so much for the wonderful journey! Today, I manage my own consulting company of Creative Excellence Management Solutions, LLC (CEMS). Starting in 2008 this firm will help businesses improve performance by using motivational training workshops, efficient work processes and thus, facilitate dignified human resource management (HRM). Moreover, CEMS, LLC will use innovation to help companies generate profitability, resource development and overall business success.

Please route questions or comments to:


Creative Excellence Management Solutions, LLC

8343 Roswell Rd

Suite #405

Atlanta, GA  30350

Phone/Fax: (404) 459-6641

CreativeExc@aol.com


Another reason to show up for work in the morning is having a *great boss*.

# CHAPTER 7

# *Profile of a Good Boss*

Many companies are successful because they choose intelligent, creative, and hardworking employees. Such individuals provide a level of excellence that makes their boss look good. What if you could choose your boss? Which resumés would you consider? Would you place value on an energetic work environment? What about your personal retirement? Would it be important to receive recognition and compensation for the value your knowledge brings to the business? Would any of the following qualities rate the top of your list? The following bosses made it to the top of the list. In one facet or more, these individuals achieved the above resumé. Please note the *brilliance* that transformed these job candidates into extraordinary heroes.

# Best Bosses' Resume

## EDUCATION

Ethical Business and Financial Management
Diversity Education
Organizational Leadership
Communication Skill and Human Motivation

## SKILLS

- Accomplished in promoting and *delegating with respect*
- Accustomed to *facilitating growth and new opportunities* for employees
- Bountiful *humility* in sharing credit
- Consistent *character and dignity* under pressure
- First-class *team leader*
- Masterful *listening* to employees
- Outstanding *teaching, mentoring, and coaching*
- Talent for displaying *gratitude and appreciation* for all
- Outstanding example of a *strong work ethic*

## ACCOMPLISHMENTS

Assisted one hundred or more employees procure job satisfaction, outstanding job performance, marketability, and other objectives of life *while building* a successful business

## Value Your Employees

*"He exhibited the courage to value, mentor, and coach."*

**Mr. Keith C. Martin** is the son of a firefighter. Like my husband, a firefighter, he never lacked the willingness to express himself. The way he did so proved to be impressive. He cared enough to declare that you are an ace and always tried to exalt you, even if you never sought such prestige. He always displayed the courage to stand up and tell everybody about your strengths and why he appreciated you. It was his custom to put such appreciation in writing so you would not feel neglected. Have you ever had a boss tell you what you deserved? Well, Mr. Keith C. Martin was such a boss. When I applied for a position with Clayton County, I was basically looking for something temporary or part-time. For a skilled worker, most bosses will gladly provide a competitive salary. However, have you ever had a boss take the initiative of outlining what you needed to live? Well, after a few months, Mr. Martin approached me with the offer of a full-time position, saying, "We need to find a way to make you permanent. You deserve all the benefits of a county employee for the future to come!"

Mr. Martin is also an innovator, and as such, he exercised a participative style of leadership. A great deal of his respect may have resulted from raising daughters of his own. He never failed to honor and consider all ideas. His love for information systems fueled my passion for the field of technology. He is a great teacher.

In today's world, many fear sharing knowledge or helping others to grow. The response you get from individuals is "Oh, look it up on the Internet" or "Read a book." I have never agreed with that type of training. The best teachers give of themselves, take time to design practical training programs, and coach you along the way. Mr. Martin was that type of teacher. If you wanted to learn, he would stop and show you how to do it. To him, knowledge was something to be shared in order to promote growth among employees. These are very simple courtesies that make all the difference in the world. He provided a powerful reason to show up for work in the morning.

## Initiate Honor of Others

*"Every assistant needs a boss that rewards her 'Just because.'"*

Most people need to have a celebration or special occasion to say, "Good job, well done," or "We appreciate you!" **Brian Johnston** was not confined by these philosophies. Often I would tell this incredible boss about my favorite dishes. Sometime later, I would find a spontaneous employee reward in the form of a gift certificate on my desk with the words "Just because." Mr. Johnston was outstanding, not only because of his heart, but also due to his uniqueness as a team player. You would never hear Brian say, "It is not my job!" In fact, I appreciated the way he and his trial team partner listened and allowed me to offer suggestions to simplify team requirements, creating reference manuals, and also, they would even jump in and help me complete my job, thereby decreasing work for the other legal assistants. What a relief it was to have these superstars in my corner. How many bosses are like that?

Another reason we all appreciated Brian was because he treated all like gold *every day*. Although he is a very accomplished attorney, intelligent, and witty, he never made us feel like second-class citizens. On a daily basis, we receive nothing less than respect. He took time to listen to the aspects of life that are important to us. Lastly, before embarking on the new day, he always gave us a hearty big laugh. No doubt, he is still providing a positive reason for other employees to show up in the morning.

## Show Appreciation

*"She rewarded her assistant in a manner of her choice."*

Some bosses may run out and get you a last-minute gift, one in which they have not put much thought into, or nothing at all. **Rebecca Benefield** proved to be different by cultivating the habit of taking me to the restaurant of my choice just because I loved it. During times when she had a tight schedule, I would suggest, "Maybe we can go another day." However, Rebecca would always insist, "Oh no! We're going today because you deserve it!" This leader did not put people off; she placed them first. In addition, she taught me a lot about law and the research thereof. On a number of days, we talked about the importance of broadening our horizons. For example, she would say, "Cynthia, there are so many other things you would be great at. Let us talk about a few." Having a great teacher and friend definitely motivated me to get up in the morning.

## Be a Mentor

*"Cynthia wanted to learn, so I felt compelled to teach her."*

When I first arrived in the legal field, I remember the face of **Linda Lovett**, senior administrator of the SGO. After I walked through that front door, I saw her standing there, smiling, ready to walk me through the new experience every step of the way. Like all great leaders, she was always a champion for me whether I was present or not. She taught me everything from the beginning to the end. I adored her like an adopted mom, and we are still good friends to this day. What made Linda especially effective was her keen sense of people skills. She dispensed a daily dose of personal interest to the entire staff. One could consider her the resident cheerleader, so to speak. She and Mr. Martin both helped me to learn what could have been a very challenging job within a matter of months; they made it a piece of cake. They gave me a great incentive to show up for work in the morning.

*Lead Your Team*

*"We worked on the most efficient team at the SGO,*
*or so we always claimed."*

**Tasha Mosley** was an excellent team leader and expeditious manager. She had a custom of preparing for court three to four weeks ahead of time. Rarely would you hear Tasha say, "*You* need to do this," or "*You* need to do that," or "I need *you* to do these extra things." The main tools she requested were the daily calendars. After that, she took all files, locked herself in the office, and returned phone calls. Extra work was completed by this leader. She always said, "You have enough to do." Because she was proactive, she helped me to focus on other responsibilities aside from those expected from a legal assistant. What I appreciate most was her routine of coming in a few minutes earlier to discuss the most important matters. If she could not be present, she would call. I consider her a rare and wonderful person. Ms. Mosley is so intelligent she could have become a leading engineer or scientist, yet she wanted to practice law, and she is excellent at doing so! Ms. Mosley was a great coach, both publicly and privately. Her example gave me a reason to show up for work.

*Show Respect*

*"She marched to the beat of a different drummer."*

**Shalonda Jones** was a new top-notch prosecutor straight out of law school. She brought an appealing attitude to the office. This person was open to all suggestions and grew to another level. How I admired her ability to take time each day to communicate and converse with you about life. Whenever I faced school projects, she took the time to hear me out and present her perspectives. In addition, she was interested in my experiences within the Brazilian community.

The most excellent quality was her courage to be openly honest with you. For the longest of times, I tried to convince her she was my superior. However, because she honored you so much, she could hardly ever see you as a subordinate. I can still remember her saying, "Cynthia, you know it is quite possible that you might just be a little overqualified to be a legal assistant." She always thinks others are capable of much more. Her perspective on things brought laughs on a daily basis. Ms. Jones is now working for the defense side of the law within her own law firm of Harris & Jones, Attorneys-at-Law, in Jonesboro, Georgia, along with her partner, Twilla Harris.

## Communicate with Dignity

*"She shared her elegance with those around her."*

**Clara Bucci** is a dignified person to work with. I loved the way she would come in early to get her work done. Although she possessed a measure of power, she never felt the need to enforce that power over your head. As a defense attorney and later prosecutor, she remained a wonderful person. Sometimes you meet people who graduate from college that then feel they know it all. Clara, on the other hand, always maintained a sense of humility. Her manner of communicating conveyed dignity and respect for all people. She would even request your advice. Would not a boss like this motivate you to show up for work in the morning? Ms. Bucci now works for the Prosecuting Attorney's Council of Georgia, an outstanding group of people. On a daily basis, they plan and provide positive support to prosecutors throughout Georgia. How amazing to have a multitude of great coaches, teachers, and mentors at your disposal. All give prosecutors the tools required to assist the public. No doubt, Ms. Bucci continues to elegantly display humility, dignity, and respect for all people.

## Show Discernment

*"She knew when you needed to talk."*

When **Mrs. Leslie Miller Terry** first arrived, she was always forthcoming with compliments regarding her fellow worker's accomplishments. She has a unique perception for people. For example, she can look at your face and tell when you need to talk. On one particular day, there was an office full of people standing in her office. I ran in rather quickly and was preparing to run out. Before I could exit, she looked at me and told everyone, "OK, that is all fine and good, but right now, I need to talk to Cynthia. Could everyone please give us privacy, please?" Great observation, Mrs. Terry! When I later chose to pursue an opportunity, she left the door open for my return, if I so desired. Thanks for the kind words and taking out time to *really* listen to your employee.

## Why Are These Bosses Outstanding?

According to *Roget's Thesaurus*, a boss can be described as a director, overseer, controller, kingpin, head honcho, etc. Although these qualities will get the job done, these qualities did not make the previously mentioned bosses significant. What made these individuals special was their good character, thoughtfulness, and frankness. Most job descriptions do not ask for these qualities. However, when they chose to bring these qualities to their position, this move transformed them into leaders.

The best managers are not only intelligent, they also possess a huge amount of experience and an even greater degree of humility. These qualities prevent their loss of focus brought on by needless power trips. Such individuals work side by side with you as team players. You could walk out the door knowing that come what may, they will handle the situation for you. There were so many other heroes like **Kim Gross**, **Janet-Smith Taylor**, **Darlene Riggins**, and more. As mentioned earlier, if I were to name them all, this book would continue into eternity.

# CHAPTER 8

# *Seven Steps to Successfully Mentor Others*

## Seven Steps to Successfully Mentor Others

1. Cultivate passion for people

2. Lead by listening

3. Treat people with dignity and respect

4. Become a go-getter

5. Invest in your employees

6. Fan the flame

7. Don't become the mummy

# 1. Cultivate Passion for People

Do you remember how you felt when you first walked in an office for an interview? I was happy to find a great job with good benefits! I was thankful for the opportunity to learn about a new field with the hope of being of true assistance to the public. As mentioned in the beginning of the book, I promised myself that I would never aspire to be part of the numerous comedies and jokes about how government offices supposedly treated the public. My goal was to take professional service to a higher level.

Why is it important we never lose that initial fervor? We do not want to become guilty of failing to give the best customer service. Nor do we want to lack the will to think out of the box and choose the best decision for the client or citizen. Lastly, we never want to lack the eagerness to do the research required to serve people with dignity and in the appropriate manner. These qualities are staples for outstanding employees in public service.

So are you still passionate about *people*? Do you still have the desire to help people? Is it still important to provide time for the victims? Do you still continue to go beyond to *really* help the public? Are you still glad to be of service?

All have different responsibilities and levels of service. Nevertheless, we are all here for the same purpose. All should be concerned about the same goal: *a person well served!* Therefore, all should support one another. As we win with employees, we win with the public by serving them well. What is the key to surviving and thriving? Cultivating a passion for people.

## 2. Lead by Listening

Once, while working at a medical facility, I learned a lesson in the importance of listening that I shall never forget. The patients were the best part of the job because they were very loving. Some were so sick I wondered if that was the last time I would see them. On one particular day, I noticed an elderly couple exhausted and ready to leave after enduring an endless number of tests. How I wanted to facilitate their return home! When I approached the superior to get his signature, he did not want to be disturbed, especially since he was in the middle of a conversation with a colleague. His example underscored the importance of listening to the people that do the work. We don't have eyes behind our heads; we surely don't possess bionic ears. An employee might catch something very important that the superior failed to notice. If you can notice their clues, you might just help the public and receive the bonus of making yourself and your department look good.

Out of the whole group, we did have one leader who felt a huge amount of compassion for people. Not only did he devote time to listen to their concerns, but also, when he lost a patient, he needed an audience to listen as he told you about this individual who was not just a part of statistics, but a wonderful person. Here we have yet another reason to get up and go to work in the morning.

## 3. Treat People with Dignity and Respect

Who deserves dignity? Should we only dignify CEOs and high officials? Of course not. If we genuinely treat people with the dignity and respect we desire for ourselves, we will honor others. By keeping this attitude, we will not lose the reason and motivation for this choice of career: *public* service.

During all my years working for Clayton, people have always told me their stories of how they were treated in other places. I will never forget my experience of renewing my car tags; this story would not be filed under the section labeled Positive. Failing to remember the situation would mean forgetting to serve people with dignity. True, no one is perfect and sometimes we aren't at the top of our game, but when our goal is to strive to be of benefit to the public and surprise them with an unexpected quality of service, everyone wins. All of the best teachers and mentors at the county showed this attitude. Many citizens left the office with tears of surprise and joy because they did not expect such dignity. I always told them, "I don't know how you were treated everywhere else, but we're going to dignify you here."

From the very first moment you walk into the door of the Clayton Courthouse, you are welcomed with an uncommon hospitality from the bailiffs, domestic engineers, legal assistants, administrative assistants, law clerks, clerks of court, prosecutors, and judges. Returning for a visit reminds me of returning home. There are special people there that will always welcome you with kind words as they continue to adhere to that higher standard of making it feel like home. Yes, a good reason to get up and go to work in the morning

## 4. Become a Go-getter

Have you ever had an employee you could count on come what may? One that does not mind arriving first in the morning just to make sure the work is done? Well, when I worked at the court the magistrate court of Clayton County had **Sue Leary**. How many courthouses can you call at 7:00 a.m. and get a *cheerful* body *glad* to be of service? This is the quality of service Ms. Leary gave to the public everyday. Throughout all my twelve years of working with the county, Sue was known for going above and beyond to be of service to the public.

Now that I have ventured into private practice, I consider her service invaluable. For Sue, it does not matter how bad the day transpired, how many defendants had to be processed, or how many times the phone would ring; she is glad to do it. Ms. Leary is a team player who provides an incredible amount of refreshment every day.

## 5. Invest in Your Employees

Outsourcing is commonplace in many businesses. In fact, when an employer wants to become more innovative or progressive, they will seek advice outside the organization. This is a great idea *if* no innovation exists within. However, what if you have employees with a wealth of experience and knowledge? Sometimes we have all the tools we need, but do we use the tools we have? You have right-arm people within your midst. Invest in them.

The best employers do what is best for themselves and *all other employees.* One thing I loved about working for Clayton is the way my supervisors always outlined the "buy-ins," meaning the incentives, fringe benefits, and rewards of a county employee. Some of the benefits were those of retirement, yearly training conferences, sit-ins on interviews for new legal assistants (or receptionists), and requesting employee's opinions in problem solving. All of these are ways to develop employees, provide a sense of family, and grow to new levels of professionalism. For its long-term survival, profitability, and positive image, a company must recognize the potential of every employee.

## 6. Fan the Flame

The most successful managers are people-focused. These heroes take time to determine what motivates their people. What will keep them happy and excited about their jobs? These individuals work hard to create a learning environment so employees can continue to grow and maintain their marketability. They do not just leave it to the employees to find their way.

Because these managers are concerned with quality, they create training routines to help employees achieve their best. This builds the confidence of the employees in the sense that they do not have to keep running back asking questions; they have a map to find the answers on their own. An individual can actually perform the job and then move on to other things.

Sometimes managers become exasperated with their employees because they do not fulfill expectations. The next time you feel exasperated, ask your employees, "Do you have the support and resources to focus on quality? Are we using your skills to the full? Does the workload need to be restructured?" If we would take inventory of our employees, we can put them in areas where they can be most productive. By doing so, we will give employees yet another reason to show up and perform a good job! We will not have temporary place fillers, but employees who will demonstrate their loyalty to the company by going above and beyond what is expected of them for their coworkers and superiors.

## 7. Don't Become the Mummy

My husband works as a firefighter in Georgia. I will never forget his training for good customer service. They use a video training program from CRM Learning called "An Invisible Man Meets the Mummy." What does this illustration mean? Well, sometimes we can become so wrapped up in our job and ourselves we forget about the people standing at the window or waiting on the phone or the person working beside you. People can actually become invisible to us if we fail to give them the quality service they deserve. We could become focused on what we are eating for lunch, a call from a boyfriend, or a bad mood that quality service for internal and external customers suffers.

All of the above excuses are irrelevant. When we walk through the front door of the office—regardless of what kind of day we are having and no matter what happened last night—the public expects us to *be professionals*. Therefore, we should always strive to give them the dignity they are worthy of.

# CHAPTER 9

# *Your Daily Checklist*

Authentic leaders are people who refuse to forget where they came from. *True heroes* of public service arrived in this place because of a passion for people. Actively listening to others provides a profound level of focus and understanding of people. One way to maintain this passion and awareness is by conducting a self-analysis. Here is your daily checklist. When you find yourself irritated, sidetracked, or distracted by something that has no reference to *helping* the public, please pull this out and ask yourself the questions therein.

# Your Daily Checklist

So how do you listen? Rate yourself on a scale from 1 to 10.

_____ 1. Do I quickly acknowledge the presence of *all* citizens, coworkers, or employees?
_____ 2. Can I put my work aside and *really* hear others out?
_____ 3. Have I asked my boss or employees how they would like to be honored? Have I cared enough to do so?
_____ 4. Did I ask the public how I could better use my privilege to serve them?
_____ 5. Have I sent a positive card to a citizen, client, or teammate enduring a challenging time?
_____ 6. Am I ready to greet the public with a smile?
_____ 7. Can I step outside of my box and strive for a higher level of service?

### TOTAL SCORE

**60-70** Excellent listening and leadership skills!
**40-60** You are 50 percent on the way to leadership
**1-30** Great initiative! Keep making progress.

## Pitfalls to Avoid

_____ 1. Failure to acknowledge a team player's presence
_____ 2. Regular preoccupation with your own concerns to the exclusion of others
_____ 3. Neglecting the procurement of feedback from *all* employees
_____ 4. Calling a meeting *only* when there is a problem
_____ 5. Criticizing suggestions of colleagues and the public while making a special effort to do so in front of others
_____ 6. Failure to strive for dignified public service

Ask yourself, "So how did I do *today*? Was I a hero for someone else? Did I strive to be an ethical leader? Is there room for improvement?" If there is, here is one more important question: How much respect would a person merit that treated you in such a manner? A good leader needs to have *genuine* support of the people they serve. Where would the business leaders be without these talented people doing the work? Leadership in action is exhibited when these individuals adhere to a custom of prioritizing weekly lunches with their direct assistant and staff, gather ideas, promote good rapport, and convey their appreciation consistently and specifically.

If a manager lacks these skills, I highly recommend a course in mastering the art of listening. Such information conveys the importance of being a team player, taking one person at a time, and honoring all differences. It will show you *how* to be a leader.

By applying positive suggestions, you *will* succeed. No matter how crowded your desk may become, how full the lobby grows, or how often the telephone rings, one will not be *defeated* by chaos. Quite often, chaos overwhelms us, causing inefficiency, thus losing you time and money. The goal is to become superefficient while giving people the focus they need and deserve. Working together to achieve a higher standard will exceed the customer or public's expectations and propel your company to unanticipated levels.

# CHAPTER 10

# *Make the Other Person's Day!*

All of the people in this book are incredible heroes because they were willing to give of themselves and help the people around them become the best. They gave knowledge to the audience that desired it. These heroes were willing to slow down and help others to grow.

Recently I spoke with one of my first coaches within the county. I asked her, "When I worked for the county, why didn't I just pretend I didn't know anything? My job would have been a lot easier." She said, "That is true, but I know you could never live by that level of service." So I thought, *How would the minimum job performance help my team and department advance? Would I really dignify people who came to us for service? What if I was on the receiving side, would this attitude dignify me?* After considering these questions, I agreed with her. Wow, she's right! The room for improvement is a great place to be. It gives you an opportunity every day to grow and improve on your level of service. What a positive contribution to yourself and society as a whole.

Sometimes we can easily become so focused on landing a position, making money, or gaining prestige that we can easily forget to build a life. Additionally, we may minimize the importance and incentives of living an ethically good life across the board. The next time we feel like holding back from giving the appropriate commendation or assistance to the people who deserve it, let us courageously move beyond ourselves and help people.

This poem always helped me to redirect my focus on service. What a great tool to acquire the proper and healthy perspective of helping people. Some may think about this poem when they are trying to come to an ethical decision. Well, Dale Wimbrow's poem resonates in my mind when I think about running an ethical business to benefit employees, customers, and society.

# The Guy in the Glass
## by
## Dale Wimbrow

When you get what you want in your struggle for self,
And the world makes you King for a day,
Then go to the mirror and look at yourself,
And see what that guy has to say.

For it isn't your Father, Mother, or Wife,
Who judgement upon you must pass.
The feller whose verdict counts most in your life
Is the guy staring back from the glass.
He's the feller to please, never mind all the rest,
For he's with you clear up to the end,
And you've passed your most dangerous, difficult test
If the guy in the glass is your friend.

You may be like Jack Homer and "chisel" a plum,
And think you're a wonderful guy,
But the man in the glass says you're only a bum
If you can't look him straight in the eye.

You can fool the whole world down the pathway of
years,
And get pats on your back as you pass,
But your final reward will be heartaches and tears
If you've cheated the man in the glass.

*Every day*, may we all look beyond ourselves by mentoring, coaching, and cheering on our teammates in the workplace. May we honor and care for people and confer to others the same degree of dignity that we would desire for ourselves. Individually we may feel we cannot accomplish that much. One legal assistant would always ask, "What can lil' ole me do?" However, a group can accomplish amazing things. How so? When you have a boss willing to stand up for you and support your goals, a team player rolling up their sleeves to pull for you and help you get the job done, or a colleague striving and standing there beside you to cheer you on, and, most important, when *you* are willing to rise to the occasion to support them all, what will this combination create? Together all forge one strong fist of success for your business and the community.

Companies can have highly effective employees, businesses, and positive work environments. The outcome we want requires us to look around and see the heroes leading, working beside us, and coaching us every day to reach our full potential and achieve success for our business.

As I stated from the beginning, "The teachers and the mentors at the county made my work experience with government agencies rewarding. By paving the way for new employees, they became incredible heroes. Such heroes created a win for the office and the public."

So here it is! This is your opportunity to set a higher standard. Hopefully, your legacy will read something like this:

Today, I went the distance for a citizen, client, or a colleague. After lunch, I surprised my boss with a thank-you card for a job well done. Tomorrow, I plan to treat my entire staff to a surprise appreciation breakfast just because they deserve it. Lastly, as a manager, I encouraged a top-notch employee to complete their education and provided my support by agreeing to provide tuition reimbursement. This is my place in history today.

May we always strive to make a real difference in the workplace by making a positive impact on the lives of people we have been privileged enough to serve. People will continue to say what they want about county employees. I will always carry the innovative words of one manager with me: "May no one in this department ever say we do things this way because we have always done them that way." If a better and smarter way to work and serve people existed, this leader challenged us to find it. Always remember, you have an opportunity every day to create a positive and unique legacy. Because I worked shoulder to shoulder with genuine heroes, my stories and experiences are very positive.

So what will your level of service recommend? When the public, customer or a teammate departs from your office or phone, will you leave them with a fair amount of dignity? Maybe a higher standard of professionalism?

The goal is to make the day of the person standing in front of you or conversing with you over the phone or the innovative boss who so effectively led you to a higher place or the coworkers who performed as a team with you. All of these heroes are waiting to cheer you on, pat you on the back, inspire you, work as a team to help dignify the public, or customer and give you the most powerful reason for showing up to your place of work tomorrow morning.

## The End

# ACKNOWLEDGMENTS

Thank you, Mr. Martin, for choosing to hire and train me. You gave me access to the world of public service and the *honor* to dignify the public or people everyday. Furthermore, thank you for never allowing me to forget my value to the department. Thank you, Ms. Terry, for understanding my desire to grow as a legal-business professional and achieve other important objectives in life. Lastly, I appreciate your extending the invitation to return if the new venture did not succeed as planned.

My appreciation extends for the untiring support of the entire staff of the Solicitor General's Office of Clayton County, Georgia, for kindly allowing me to honor and dignify them for their daily hard work.

A world of thanks to Jennifer Smith for her outstanding job and participation in the team. You are the best!

To Frank Smith, my outstanding attorney, who took time to read the book and convey his appreciation for the value of professionalism for any person.

Appreciation also extends to Steve Frey, Steve Lister, and Leon Hicks, who have shown excellent encouragement and shared wonderful stories since our first acquaintance back in 1993.

Grateful am I for the encouragement and support of Talya Blazia, an outstanding legal assistant, and for the law firm of George Creal.

I will always remember the kind encouragement from incredible stories of Mark Pittman, Tyrone Walls, Ed Collins, Thomas Gillespie, Carl Freeman, Darell Martin, Ernest Nesmith and the late Scott Harrison. Thank you for being so wonderful to me.

A note of appreciation to Brenda Smith, Clerk of the State court, who has always remained a champion of positive ideas for the county, the public in general, and me.

Thanks to Evelyn Proctor Sandefur, for filling in the blanks. When I first arrived to legal field, I had a wealth of questions. You never made me feel clueless.

My gratitude goes out to the domestic engineers of Clayton County. These individuals always faced the day with a smile and a gentle word of encouragement and appreciation. Keep up the fine work!

Thanks to the self-publishing company of Xlibris for showing such patience and insight as we pieced together the puzzle of this fabulous story of incredible people.

Much appreciation to my mentors, who have shown fine examples of humility, leadership, teamwork for outstanding business expertise today.

A million words of gratitude for Mr. Michael P. Baird for being such a good coach, not only throughout my legal career, but during the final completion of the book.

Lastly, a round of applause for *all* employees and individuals, past and present, who go the distance daily to make another person's day in Clayton County, Georgia.

With sincere appreciation,

Cynthia A. Jenkins

# REFERENCES

CRM Learning. 1994. *The Invisible Man Meets the Mummy*. http://www.crmlearning.com/invisible-man-meets-the-mummy-government-version.

McCutcheon, M. 1998. *Roget's Super Thesaurus*. Cincinnati, OH: Writer's Digest Books.

Wimbrow, Dale. 1934. "The Guy in the Glass." http://www.theguyintheglass.com/gig.htm.

www.ingramcontent.com/pod-product-compliance
Lightning Source LLC
Chambersburg PA
CBHW021233280526
45784CB00005B/2087